ABANDONED
KENTUCKY

Sherman Cahal • Adam Paris • Michael Maes

MacIntyre Purcell Publishing Inc.

MacIntyre Purcell Publishing Inc.
194 Hospital Rd.
Lunenburg, Nova Scotia
B0J 2C0
(902) 640-3350

www.macintyrepurcell.com
info@macintyrepurcell.com

Printed and bound in Canada by Friesens

Cover design: Denis Cunningham
Book design: Denis Cunningham

On the cover: Falls of Rough Mill and dam along the Rough River in Breckinridge County. See page 18 for more information.

ISBN: 978-1-77276-171-9

Library and Archives Canada Cataloguing in Publication

Title: Abandoned Kentucky / Sherman Cahal, Adam Paris & Michael Maes.
Names: Cahal, Sherman, author, photographer. | Paris, Adam, author, photographer. | Maes, Michael
  (Photographer), author, photographer.
Identifiers: Canadiana 20220204047 | ISBN 9781772761719 (hardcover)
Subjects: LCSH: Abandoned buildings—Kentucky—Pictorial works. | LCSH: Ruined buildings—Kentucky—
  History—Pictorial works. | LCSH: Kentucky—History, Local—Pictorial works. | LCGFT: Illustrated
  works.
Classification: LCC F452 .C34 2022 | DDC 976.90022/2—dc23

This book is dedicated to J. Winston Coleman, Jr.,
a noted author and historian
whose photographs and descriptions of antebellum residences,
country churches, and other significant places of yesteryear
have provided much inspiration and guidance.

Drive along any Kentucky back road and a Methodist church with a bright red door can be spotted, even if it's been abandoned for a number of years such as this sanctuary near Union Star. Simply, the red door is the symbolism of Christians entering into worship, into the presence of God, through the blood of Christ.

Introduction

The Commonwealth of Kentucky, rich in history and heritage, is defined by its endless farm fields of the Jackson Purchase, the sprawling horse farms in the Bluegrass region, and the winding mountains of Appalachia. In between the countryside, wayside communities and large cities is a diverse landscape marked by stately antebellum residences, forlorn distilleries, vintage schoolhouses, grand theaters, underground mines and industrial giants.

Kentucky has undergone numerous transformations over its 230 years of existence and the only constant over time has been change.

The coal industry, which formerly dominated the state's economy and politics, is a shell of its former self, a victim of mechanization that relies on far fewer workers, environmental concerns, the decline of the domestic steel industry, and the rise of natural gas and renewable power generation. The bourbon whiskey industry, which was all but decimated during the growing temperance movement that led to the national prohibition on alcohol in the 1920s and 1930s, was able to slowly rebound. Hemp and tobacco, once mainstays in agricultural fields, along with their associated processing plants, were depleted by shifting attitudes and federal regulations. And large integrated steel mills, which relied on the mass consumption of pig iron, limestone and coke to charge a blast furnace to produce molten iron, have largely been replaced by more lean and efficient electric arc furnaces that rely on scrap metal and direct reduced iron or pig iron.

Likewise, grand, opulent residences that once housed generations of families under one roof withered under societal changes. Churches that once preached to the masses have in many areas closed down under shrinking congregations because of shifts in beliefs, population losses and other external factors. And schools that were once the backbone of every community have been consolidated into large, sterile and anonymous campuses that serve a much larger geographical region.

Much along the lines of J. Winston Coleman, Jr., who over the period of decades collected hundreds of photographs and narratives of historic places in the Commonwealth for his weekly features in the *Lexington Herald-Leader*, this book is the culmination of personal endeavors of three photographers that involved traveling thousands of miles to nearly every hilltop and hollow, and countless hours of research.

A few of the locations profiled in *Abandoned Kentucky* have known histories and stories, but for many others, little is known other than what can be visually interpreted and inferred. The book is but a placeholder in time that showcases beauty in decay.

(Above) The Columbia Theatre was furnished in pastel shades of green, pink, tan, and blue, the woodwork finished in an antique grey, and the columns and ornaments outlined in gold leaf. The walls were originally adorned with six paintings of Kentucky nature scenes painted by Louisville artists, while the ceiling contained an art glass installation.

(Opposite) The Columbia Theatre was one of the finest theaters in downtown Paducah. Developed by Leo F. Keiler, the 2,000-seat facility opened in April 1927 and was extensively renovated with steel and bronze decorative sconces in 1952. The Columbia closed in 1987 and efforts are currently underway to restore the facility as a performing arts venue.

The Little Union Baptist Church in McLean County was a church for Blacks that was organized after April 1870. By 1960, there were less than a dozen members at Little Union and the church closed around 1973 when the last remaining members went elsewhere to attend services. The Little Union Baptist Church building was reused by a Pentecostal congregation in 1975 until it moved to a new building in 1980.

Situated atop Farmer Ridge in Arvel at the junction of Jackson, Lee, and Owsley counties is an abandoned one-room church that was later converted for use as a residence. Arvel was originally referred to as Old Orchard for its vast groves of apple trees.

This circa 1825 clapboard-sided residence, tucked away in the hills of Lee County, was home to the Snowden family. Dudley Bishop Snowden, one of the children who lived at the house, served as the postmaster for the local community. The post office was located in the rear of the house.

Despite cracking and delamination of the plaster, much of the Snowden House remains intact after decades of disuse.

The Columbia Mantel Company was a mantel and furniture factory in Louisville. The city's location along the Ohio River and its mid-19th century population boom spurred the development of large furniture manufacturers after the conclusion of the Civil War. By the 1870s, the city was home to five significant furniture factories. Columbia Mantel originally produced mantels before expanding into furniture production.

Fisher's Travel Camp was a roadside stop for travelers along U.S. Route 25 in Scott County, offering weary travelers fuel, southern cooking, and lodging. It opened in 1928 by Tom and Hallie Fisher and flourished until the development of Interstate 75 in the early 1960s siphoned much of the traffic from the highway.

Although it looks like fashionable shiplap, the horizontally-laid pine boards comprise part of the basic structure of this derelict house in rural Casey County.

Tucked away deep in the desolate farmlands along the Ohio River in Oldham County is a well-preserved farmhouse with vintage furnishings.

(**Left**) Sometimes there isn't much to photograph inside an abandoned house. In this case, the only color and interest from this dilapidated house in Larue County came from these two vivid, vinyl-topped chairs set against patterned wallpaper in a kitchen.

(**Opposite**) Remnants of a once prosperous dairy farm remain nearly intact near Owensboro. Just 40 years ago, there were 265,000 dairy cows dotting 2,000 family farms across the Commonwealth, but that number has dramatically declined today to just 45,000 dairy cows on just 850 farms. A combination of factors has led to the downturn, including a long-term reduction in milk consumption, higher input costs, and the rise of large-scale industrial farms and processing plants.

(Above) The sawmill along the Rough River in Breckenridge County closed in 1933 after all of the nearby trees had been timbered and processed but the gristmill operated until 1965. Falls of Rough Mill was in a state of collapse by the close of the 20th century. Much of the original equipment from its sawmill and gristmill operations remained inside. After decades of abandonment, Falls of Rough Mill collapsed into the Rough River on August 14, 2016.

(Opposite) Willis Green II, the son of a prominent early settler in Danville and a lawyer and surveyor in Hardinsburg, erected the sawmill, gristmill, and dam along the Rough River in Breckinridge County in 1823. A small community developed around his mill and it was named Falls of Rough in 1850 after the nearby rapids.

Late evening light bathes the former Washington County Coon Club building near Springfield. Raccoon hunting for meat and fur with specially bred dogs is as old as the Commonwealth itself with many counties boasting an active coon hunting club.

Not much but walls remain of Duncan Hall along Route 55 near Bloomfield. The antebellum Federal-style residence was built by Major Green Duncan who served in the state legislature and as a sheriff for Nelson County, as well as a depot agent for the Louisville & Nashville Railroad's Bloomfield Branch. The house was abandoned in the early 1990s. A lightening s trike on August 2, 2009, sparked a fire that engulfed the entire residence in flames.

(**Opposite**) A Ford van and truck remain outside a still standing but increasingly obscured residence near Cloverport in Breckinridge County.

(**Above**) Seemingly, some of the old wood clapboard siding on this house in Hancock County has been scavenged for other uses.

"There are no unsacred places; there are only sacred places and desecrated places."

— Wendell Berry (Given), poet, novelist, and environmentalist

A vintage Electrolux vacuum, with a steel and aluminum canister, and woven cloth and aluminum hose, quietly rests on the floor of a church abandoned along the Licking River in Mason County.

Inside an otherwise non-descript house in Oldham County was a retro kitchen outfitted with a Youngstown Kitchens line, including porcelain enameled steel cabinets and steel stamped glazed sinks. The kitchen set was made by Mullins Manufacturing Corporation.

Old Crow Distillery was a straight bourbon whiskey distillery along Glenn's Creek near Frankfort. The brand was introduced in 1935 by James C. Crow and became one of the top selling bourbon drinks in the nation. Here, a Spring House provides limestone enriched spring water that is essential to bourbon production. The limestone adds minerals like calcium, while filtering out impurities such as iron. It also has a high pH, which promotes fermentation.

(**Left**) Worn sandstone steps lead to an entrance adorned with cast iron and covered windows at the former machine room for the Schaefer-Meyer and Frank Fehr brewery complex in the Smoketown neighborhood of Louisville. The complex was later used by Merchants Ice and Cold Storage.

(**Opposite**) Fermenting tanks remain intact inside a partly demolished building. Old Crow Distillery closed in the late 1980s after undergoing a swift decline because of a production error in the amount of setback used that negatively impacted the taste of the whiskey. (Setback is the spent mash from a previously distilled batch of whiskey added to the next batch to ensure consistency of flavor.) Portions of the complex were later scrapped of any value.

(Opposite) The first fixed crossing over the Kentucky River at Camp Nelson opened in 1838. Regarded as one of the longest of its type in the world, the 240-foot covered bridge became a major artery between the Union and the Confederates during the Civil War, with Camp Nelson playing a crucial role in defending the Union during the conflict. It was replaced by a Parker through truss bridge in 1926 and then bypassed by a new four-lane crossing in 1971.

(Above) A shuttered coal tipple remains along the Chesapeake & Ohio Railway's Long Fork Subdivision near McDowell. It was operated by the Sizemore Mining Corporation from the 1940s until 1983, and then by Old Circle Coal Company until it was idled in the mid-1980s.

(Above) Hazel Green Academy was established in 1880 as a mission for the Kentucky mountains. It offered low rates of tuition and free education for the indigent, and opened at a time when public schools were few and far between. Enrollment began to slowly decline by the 1910s because of the prevalence of state-supported schools; the Academy became financially insolvent 1983.

(Insets) Pearre Hall at Hazel Green Academy was constructed in 1901 and used as a classroom space and as a female dormitory.

Late autumn shrines around a long-abandoned, clapboard-sided house along Barrett Creek in Carter County.

(**Above**) High on a ridge above Hoods Creek along Paris Road in Clark County is a distinctive house whose lawn is seemingly used for storage of neat bales of hay.

(**Opposite**) Parting skies reveal a golden sunset at an abandoned farmhouse near the biblically-named community of Ninevah in Anderson County.

(**Above**) A simple, two-story, log-cabin house, partly concealed with clapboard siding and a leaning fieldstone fireplace, is tucked away on a working cattle farm near Law-renceburg. It has been preserved as-is for posterity.

(**Opposite**) Plaster lathe crumbles, exposing tongue board underneath, inside the formerly abandoned Holt House in rural Breckenridge County. Situated in a grove of trees on a plain, with a view of the Ohio River to the north, the Holt House was home to Judge Advocate General Joseph Holt who served in the administrations of Presidents James Buchanan, Abraham Lincoln, Andrew Johnson, and Ulysses Grant.

(Right) Discarded spindles rest in a basket adjacent to rows of antique ring spinning machines that spun fibers to produce yarn at the former January & Wood mill along Second Street in Maysville. In 1834, William Shotwell constructed a cotton mill, which was incorporated as January & Wood in 1888. The firm became known for its high-grade carpet warp, twines, and high-grade cordage.

(Opposite) At the time of its closure in 2004, the January & Wood textile mill was the oldest continuously operating business in Maysville and the oldest family-owned business in Kentucky. Demolition of the mill began in 2006 but work was halted for a year because of the presence of asbestos that had not been properly abated.

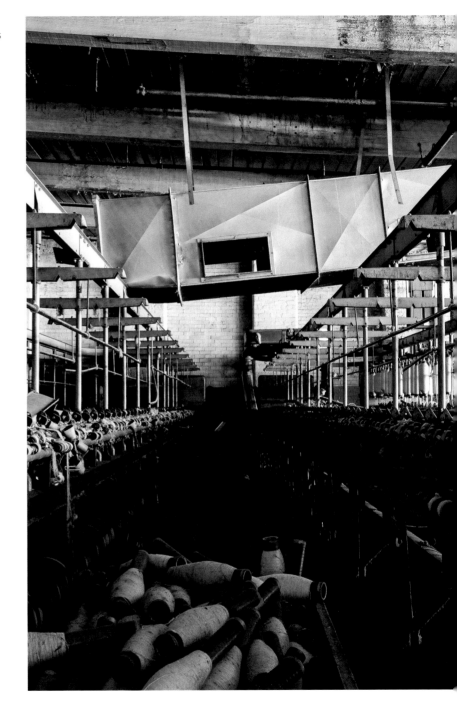

These restrooms were on the backside of the stands and were the last remaining buildings at the Ellis Speedway in western Daviess County before the land was converted back to farmland. This track started as a go-kart racing track in May 1962 and expanded, then closed around 1971. Darrell Waltrip got his start here at the age of 15.

(Above) Isolated and alone and miles from any town, a once grand farmhouse near the Green River in McLean County stands silent.

(Inset) A few remnants of prior occupants, such as this leather shoe, remain inside the old farmhouse outside of Calhoun in McLean County.

Rich, warm beadboard and trim adorn the interior of a farmhouse along the Green River in McLean County.

Although the woodwork remains intact, the interior of the farmhouse yields only a few personal artifacts and some broken furniture.

(Above) The Amanda Blast Furnace, once one of the largest in the world, stands silent as the last of the evening light wanes. Armco Steel Ashland Works, later a part of AK Steel, was an integrated steel mill that sprawled over 700 acres just west of Ashland. At its height, it featured two blast furnaces, a basic oxygen furnace, continuous caster, hot strip, coating lines, coking plant, and various finishing and coiling facilities. Steel production was idled in December 2015 and the entire plant was closed in January 2019.

(Opposite) One of Kentucky's many roadside attractions, Guntown Mountain was located near Cave City. Opened in 1969, it featured a replica of an old western town, complete with simulated gunfights and souvenirs. After closing in 2013, it briefly reopened as Funtown Mountain before relaunching as its old namesake Guntown Mountain in 2021.

(Above) Young's High Bridge was constructed over the Kentucky River between Lawrenceburg and Versailles in 1889 for the Louisville Southern Railway. At the time of its completion, it was the highest single-span cantilever structure in the world. Declining freight traffic led Louisville Southern's successor, Norfolk Southern, to mothball the line in 1985, including the aging bridge which had never been strengthened or structurally modified. The bridge is still minimally used for bungee jumping.

(Opposite) The Inland Steel Company developed a new underground coal mine at Price in 1951 to replace a depleted mine in Wheelwright. Although much of the preparation plant was demolished after the Price mine closed in 1991, the refuse conveyor, supply house, bathhouse, and office complex remain in various states of decay.

(Above) Scrap trees are virtually holding up a windblown house from entirely collapsing.

(Opposite) The distinctive blue-and-white Abel Gabbard residence was constructed at Sand Gap in Jackson County in 1890. Abel B. Gabbard, Sr. was born on February 1, 1861, in nearby Booneville and died on January 27, 1952. Abandoned for decades, portions of the house have since collapsed.

One of Kentucky's many fading communities, Union Star, was first settled around 1790. It was named for the Union Meetinghouse organized in 1845 by Thomas D. Helm, local landowner and storekeeper, and for the star-like configuration of the roads that extended from the community to neighboring towns. This long-abandoned residence stands as a silent reminder of a more prosperous past.

"A community is the mental and spiritual condition of knowing that the place is shared, and that the people who share the place define and limit the possibilities of each other's lives."

— Wendell Berry, Kentucky poet and novelist

The long-abandoned M.C. Napier High School is located in Perry County and was named after M.C. Napier who played for the Hazard Navajos from 1969 to 1973. Inside, a tribute mural to the terrorist attacks of September 11, 2001, remains intact.

Cottage Furnace operated between 1854 and 1879 along Horse Ridge in Estill County and was the first hot blast pig iron furnace in the region. Operations were suddenly ceased after the death of an owner's son. Workers neglected to tap the furnace, leaving behind a solid mass of iron in the stack that remains today.

Richwood Tahoe Railroad was a two-foot, narrow-gauge passenger railroad around Columbia Sussex's headquarters in Crestview Hills. Built by Columbia Sussex CEO Bill Yung, a railroad enthusiast, the one-sixth scale passenger railroad circled the corporate campus.

The Kentucky Union Railway, later owned by the Louisville & Nashville Railroad, once extended for 95 miles between Lexington and Jackson. Because of its rugged terrain, the line included 20 bridges and six tunnels, including a bore under Torrent. Numerous steep grades and maintenance-intensive tunnels served as a determinant for the line as a heavy coal hauling route; the railroad was abandoned in sections between 1916 and 1947.

(Opposite) The J.W.M. Field Distillery was built in 1873 near Owensboro. Prohibition dealt a major blow to many distilleries and the J.W.M. Field Distillery closed in 1929-1930. In this scene, the rickhouse at the former distillery was reused for storage.

(Above) Predating the distillery was the Field residence which was in a state of collapse after years of disuse. It was later torn down for the construction of the new Daviess County Middle School.

(Above) The Keneseth Israel Synagogue was an Orthodox sanctuary in downtown Louisville. The assembly was formed in 1926 when the B'nai Jacob and Beth Hamedrash Hagodol congregations merged.

(Opposite)The Keneseth Israel Synagogue building, designed in the Neo-Classical style by the architectural firm of Joseph & Joseph, opened in 1929. In 1964, Keneseth Israel relocated to a suburban campus and its old location was used by at least five other churches until becoming vacant in 2019. A fire ripped through the old sanctuary in March 2021 leading to its demolition later in the year.

(Above) Hidden by years of overgrowth behind a house is a circa 1953 Oldsmobile 88. The model was one of General Motors' most profitable and best performing vehicles because of its size, weight, and advanced V8 engine, and is considered by some to be the first muscle car.

(Opposite) USS *Sachem* and USS *Phenakite* is a yacht that was used by the United States Navy from 1917 to 1919 and again from 1942 to 1945. It was later used as a tour boat before becoming abandoned just yards from the Ohio River near Petersburg.

(**Opposite**) A concrete coaling tower constructed by the Louisville & Nashville Railroad remains intact over active CSX tracks in Irvington. The coaling tower used gravity to slide coal down a chute into the waiting trains' coal storage area in tender cars that were immediately behind steam locomotives. The need for coaling towers waned as railroads transitioned to diesel locomotives in the 1950s.

(**Above**) A vintage Mercedes-Benz sedan is forever parked in front of an abandoned ranch-style residence.

(Left) An antique spinning wheel used for spinning thread or yarn from fibers, remains inside a shuttered residence in Mercer County.

(Opposite) A rustic Blue Bird school bus with a Ford B series chassis is used for storage on a farm in the Salt Lick valley of Rowan County.

(Opposite) Old Lewis Hunter Distillery was a straight bourbon whiskey distillery along the South Fork of the Licking River, originally built in 1850 as the Megibben & Bramble Distillery. It became Old Lewis Hunter Distillery in 1902 and operated, except during Prohibition, until 1974.

(Above) Damron's Marathon was a staple of the Virgie community, a family-owned business where you could grab fuel, get your vehicle repaired, and strike up a friendly conversation with the shop owner.

Hidden during much of the year, an abandoned house in Nelson County seemingly pops out of a cut corn field after the fall harvest.

A traditional Colonial Revival-styled house still stands tall at the edge of a disused farm in Daviess County.

The salvaging of the wood clapboard siding at a now-demolished Methodist church in Hancock County reveals an intricate pattern of sheathing.

(Above) Parker Tobacco Company was a tobacco purchasing, processing, marketing, and commercial storage operation in Maysville. The company began a slow decline in the 1990s, aided in part because of declining smoking rates in the United States and the elimination of government quotas that hurt the company's finances. The issue was compounded when the burley cooperative refused to participate with the company over quality issues. Parker Tobacco declared bankruptcy in 1997 after a poor growing season. After the closure, machinery was kept on the premises with the plan to reopen the business as a redrying facility under Kentucky Tobacco Processors. The proposal never came to fruition.

(Opposite) A listing church standing by the wayside was once the center of the Olympia community in Bath County. Incorporated in 1882, Olympia was named for the nearby Olympian Springs and was a hub of activity between the Lexington & Big Sandy and the Owingsville & Olympia railroads.

CAUTION
MAGNETO IS NOT INTERNALLY
GROUNDED. CONSULT OWNERS
MANUAL BEFORE DISCONNECTING.

MILE HIGH
BLUE.

(**Opposite**) A circa 1976 Beechcraft C23 Sundowner 180 has rested in the weeds for decades at the lightly used Combs Field in Johnson County. The airport used to be the hub of commercial aviation activity from its dedication in 1964 until it was functionally replaced by Big Sandy Regional Airport in 1986.

(**Above**) The heading indicator, which displays the aircraft's heading of the Beechcraft C23 Sundowner 180 in compass points, shows 11° slightly northeast.

A third generation Ford F-Series truck and a Ford Fairlane remain situated outside of a barn in the foothills of the Appalachia.

A mid-century International Harvester Farmall tractor remains in front of an abandoned clapboard-sided house in Nelson County.

(**Opposite**) The distinctive Union Station depot in Henderson was constructed of brick and granite in 1901-02 at the cost of $25,000. It served the Louisville & Nashville and Illinois Central Railroads and by 1922, the facility handled 24 passenger trains daily. The rise of the automobile decimated passenger railroad operations and the Illinois Central ceased its passenger trains into Henderson in 1941. The Louisville & Nashville followed suit on in 1971.

(**Above**) A CSX freight train quickly passes by the abandoned Union Station in Henderson.

Old Taylor Distillery was a straight bourbon whiskey distillery along Glenn's Creek near Frankfort. Constructed by E.H. Taylor in 1887, Old Taylor was considered a showcase of bourbon making in the state. A peristyle spring house, sunken gardens, stone bridges, gazebos, and castle-like buildings adorned with turrets surrounded the 82-acre property, giving it a charming yet imposing composition.

Fermenting and mixing tanks were left inside Old Taylor Distillery after it closed in 1972. Inspired by photographs of the abandoned distillery, Will Arvin and Wes Murry purchased Old Taylor Distillery in 2014 and formed Castle & Key. After nearly a half-century, bourbon production has resumed on the restored grounds of Old Taylor.

"If we work upon marble, it will perish; if we work upon brass, time will efface it; if we rear temples, they will crumble into dust; but if we work upon immortal minds, if we imbue them with principles, with just fear of God and love of our fellow-men, we engrave on those tablets something which will brighten to all eternity."

— Daniel Webster, lawyer, statesman, and orator

(Opposite) Constructed circa 1880 by the King Bridge Company of Cleveland, Ohio, this unique and rare bowstring through truss bridge once carried a local route over Rock Lick Creek between Falls of Rough and Glen Dean in Breckinridge County.

The fortunes of Graham School blossomed and waned with the fortunes of the coal industry in Muhlenberg County, and eventually closed in 2004 because of low enrollment. After years of abandonment, the building was rehabilitated for use as a distillery.

A stark black-and-white captures the mood of a modest two-story house near Brandenburg on Halloween.

(Opposite) Castle Marina was once a bustling marina and retail outlet along the Ohio River near Greenup but has been closed for several years because of the owner's declining health.

(Above) Someone's dream of a houseboat lies abandoned next to Castle Marina along the Ohio River near Greenup. According to local accounts, it was once the host of numerous parties that continued into the warm summer nights.

(Above) A sunburst peeks through the branches of an aged tree that looms over an equally aged house in Shelby County.

(Opposite) Old Stanley Distillery was built by Ben F. and Thomas A. Medley in the early 1960s in Daviess County. It operated sporadically over the years and by 1970, it had produced 2,000 barrels of whiskey

(**Above**) The Fisher-Byington House was a circa 1845 antebellum residence in Danville. The two-story Greek Revival-style residence, designed by notable architect Robert Russell, Jr., was located on a small hill overlooking the Reed Farm.

(**Opposite**) The house was later vacated in anticipation that it would be converted into a funeral home, but the high costs of renovating and restoring the structure led to its eventual abandonment and destruction.

A. J. Hitt, an operator of a flour and grist mill in Millersburg, constructed an elaborate Federal-style house south of the city. It featured fine Flemish bond brickwork and extensive wood paneling. Around 1877, the house was renovated with Italianate styling by William Tarr, a farmer and distiller.

A General Electric refrigerator is all that remains inside the William Tarr house.

(Opposite) After decades of desertion, much of the William Tarr House has collapsed.

(Above) The Chesapeake & Ohio Railroad YMCA provided overnight lodging, baths, meeting space, and other accommodations for railroad workers in Russell. It declined in usage after the railroad switched to diesel locomotives instead of labor-intensive steam engines during the 1950s. The transition to diesel meant fewer stops for refueling and layovers by railroad workers, conductors, and engineers. Further mechanization of labor further reduced the railyard's workforce, and the railroad withdrew its financial support of the YMCA in 1984. The facility closed in 1992.

(Opposite) A quaint clapboard-sided building in the middle of farmland near Stanley remains as a witness to a time when education was segregated by ethnicity. The school opened circa 1912 and operated possibly until 1933. The building was later relocated to a farm and used for storage.

(Above) A house on its last legs slumps beside a set of active railroad tracks near McBrayer, a small Anderson County community named for a local family.

Completed by the TVA in 1963, Paradise Fossil Plant was one of the largest coal-fired power plants in the world. After its capacity was replaced with a natural gas-fired, combined-cycle facility, demolition of Paradise began in 2021.

The Elmer Smith Power Plant was a coal power plant in Owensboro and was built during a time of double-digit increases in the demand of power statewide and in the Southeast. Coal was mostly supplied from the Peabody Energy surface mine in Muhlenberg and at other surface mines in the western reaches of the state. The plant closed in 2020 because of costly improvements required to rehabilitate its mechanical equipment and upgrade its coal ash handling and pollution control systems; its generating capacity was replaced by coal-fired capacity elsewhere, hydropower, and solar.

Conveyors for the Gibraltar coal mine once loaded coal into awaiting barges along the Green River near Central City.

The Green River Steel Mill opened in Owensboro in 1953 at the cost of $12.5 million and at its peak, the facility employed around 600 to 700 persons. It closed permanently in 2001 and was later demolished.

(**Opposite**) A crumbling house stands silent on a hilltop farm in rural Trimble County.

(**Above**) A waning sun bathes its last light on a shack atop Brier Ridge in Spencer County.

Fitchburg Furnace, designed by Fred Fitch and constructed by masons from Ravenna, Italy along Millers Fork in Estill County, was opened by the Red River Iron Manufacturing Company in 1869. The pig-iron furnace as the largest of its type in the world with a daily tonnage output of 25 tons. The economic Panic of 1873 and the discovery of rich iron ore in Alabama caused Fitchburg to close just after producing 16,000 tons of iron.

A circa 1945 Kelvinator refrigerator and a 1940s-era Westinghouse refrigerator sit in an abandoned home in Daviess County.

Waverly Hills operated as a 400-patient tuberculosis sanatorium between 1910 and 1961 in Louisville. It featured separated patient rooms, sunrooms, and spacious rooftop recreational spaces. The development of streptomycin showed efficacy against tuberculosis and the hospital was readapted as the Woodhaven Geriatrics Center, a rest home for the elderly, between 1963 and 1981.

Meadowcrest was a mansion located on the former Meadowcrest Farm in Lexington. The thoroughbred farm was carved out of the original Hamburg Place estate in 1929, and at its center was an opulent, Georgian Revival residence that included a pine-paneled library, a hand-carved English oak fireplace brought over from a house in Surrey, England, and a flying staircase with a red carpet runner that was the same color as the racing silks of the Hamburg stable. The house was torn down in 2022 for a new mixed-use development.

(**Opposite**) A Baldwin 71 Series Orga-Sonic organ remains inside a mostly deserted house atop Yelvington. With little demand for used models that were too heavy to easily move, musical instruments such as organs and pianos were often left behind in houses.

(**Above**) Mother Nature is quickly reclaiming this house set amongst a forest in Washington County.

(Left) Surrounded by patterned floral wallpaper, an oversized chair is draped by blowing white curtains from a broken window.

(Opposite) This three-span Pratt and Parker camelback through truss bridge was built in 1894 by the Pencoyd Bridge & Construction Company and originally carried the Chesapeake & Ohio Railway (C&O) mainline across the mouth of the Big Sandy River between Catlettsburg, Kentucky, and Kenova, West Virginia. It was relocated to carry trains across the Levisa Fork along the C&O's Levisa Subdivision in Pike County. After a mine at Slones Branch Station closed in 2017, the track was no longer needed and was removed in 2021.

(Opposite) The Custer House in Ohio County is just one of many farmhouses slowly withering away in the countryside, a victim of a dying family farm and a homestead that no longer exists.

(Above) The otherwise wrecked Centertown House hides a hand-painted mural of local scenery.

Before the dawn of the automobile and the first-rate railroad, the Barren River was one of the primary routes of industry and commerce. Flatboats would be used to ship produce to New Orleans and wood to the massive sawmills in Evansville. As part of a canalization project, the state built Lock & Dam No. 1 along the Barren prior to 1886, which was rebuilt in 1934, and closed for a lack of commercial traffic in 1973.

Waning evening light filters through leaded glass in this all-but-collapsed house.

(**Above**) Everything will eventually return to the earth. This sinking house on a tobacco farm near Somerset in the southern reaches of the state has long been tilting downward because of a rotting foundation and soft soils.

(**Opposite**) The last autumn light fades on a traditional clapboard-sided house nestled under two eastern white oak trees in rural Nelson County.

(Opposite) The Cannel City Union Church was an abandoned multi-denominational church in Cannel City. The community reached its prominence in the early part of the 20th century as a company town organized by the Kentucky Block Cannel Coal Company, but after the mines were closed in 1933 because of a lack of economically viable coal reserves and the Great Depression, the town declined in vitality and population. The church lasted until 1961 when it disbanded because of a dwindling congregation.

(Right) A traditional brick residence is framed by a missing window at an adjoining building on a farm in rural Shelby County.

(**Left**) The former Merchants Ice and Cold Storage facility in the Smoketown neighborhood of Louisville was originally a part of the Schaefer-Meyer and Frank Fehr breweries that date back to 1861.

(**Opposite**) Space was at a premium inside Merchants Ice and Cold Storage facility, and compact spiral staircases connected the several floors inside various rooms.

"I thought if every teacher in every school in America—rural, village, city, township, church, public, or private, could inspire his pupils with all the power he had, if he could teach them as they had never been taught before to live, to work, to play, and to share, if he could put ambition into their brains and hearts, that would be a great way to make a generation of the greatest citizenry America ever had."

— Jesse Stuart, author *The Thread That Runs So True*

The Boston School in Butler County stands as a reminder of 19th and early 20th century education, when schools were often more than an educational institution – they anchored the community. Most have been consolidated into larger county-wide facilities in a vein to save costs, standardize school materials, and provide broader opportunities through a variety of subjects.

(Left) A small but respectable community developed around the Greenup Lime Works along the Ohio River in the 1840s. Lime from the furnace was shipped by packet boats to Pittsburg and Cincinnati. A one-room log structure tucked within Limeville Hollow served as the first school for the village, later replaced with a wood-frame building closer to the river in 1909.

(Opposite) The hotel in Union Star still remains standing decades after it last accepted guests. The community was once the crossroads of northern Breckinridge County and along a significant route between Cloverport and Brandenburg.

(**Opposite and Above**) General stores were often more than just a mercantile. They functioned as a post office and as the community's social center.

(Left) The Farmers Bank of Bourbon County was established by William F. Heathman in 1903. The modest one-story building featured an elaborate parapet across the top with the name of the bank embossed in Art Nouveau lettering. The bank closed in 1928.

(Opposite) The sun sets on an old motel and restaurant that went by a few names over the years, including Pendleton's, Payton's, and Whitey's. It was constructed by the Pendleton family in the 1940s to cater to motorists traveling along the Midland Trail between Owensboro and Henderson. The completion of the Audubon Parkway in 1970 siphoned through traffic away from the Midland Trail that caused a slow decline of the motel and ultimately led to its closure.

This partially collapsed farmhouse sits behind a winding driveway in Hancock County.

Constructed in 1963, Gabes Tower was an iconic landmark on the Owensboro skyline for decades. The 13-story mid-rise, designed by R. Ben Johnson and built by Gabe Fiorella, Sr., was home to Gabes Tower Motor Inn, a large restaurant, and a rooftop pool. After years of decline and eventual abandonment, Gabes Tower was demolished in 2020.

Prior to its rehabilitation into market-rate apartments, the upper floors at 845 Monmouth Street in central Newport were long disused. Work to renovate the units had stalled years before, leaving them in a state of partial deconstruction.

A porch swing and chairs indicates that the front porch of this abandoned house in Spencer County was once a happening place where both neighbors and friends congregated.

(Opposite) Located in Park City are the remains of Bell's Tavern. Constructed in 1830 by Col. William Bell, it served as a stagecoach stop for people traveling to Mammoth Cave. Bell's Tavern became renowned for its southern cuisine and its sweet peach and honey brandies for "Joy before the journey's end" and operated until it burned circa 1860. Work on a new stone structure was started but was halted by the Civil War.

(Right) A worn post office mailbox with an eagle emblem hung on a chain link fence endures the passing time outside of a collapsing shotgun-style house in the Portland neighborhood of Louisville.

The Photographers